CENGAGE Learning

Novels for Students, Volume 16

Project Editor: David Galens

Editorial: Anne Marie Hacht, Sara Constantakis, Ira Mark Milne, Pam Revitzer, Kathy Sauer, Timothy J. Sisler, Jennifer Smith, Daniel Toronto, Carol Ullmann **Research**: Sarah Genik

Permissions: Debra Freitas, Shalice Shah-Caldwell
Manufacturing: Stacy Melson

Imaging and Multimedia: Lezlie Light, Kelly A. Quin, Luke Rademacher **Product Design**: Pamela A. E. Galbreath, Michael Logusz © 2002 by Gale. Gale is an imprint of The Gale group, Inc., a division of Cengage Learning Inc.

Gale and Design® and Cengage Learning™ are trademarks used herein under license.

For more information, contact
The Gale Group, Inc.
27500 Drake Rd.

Farmington Hills, MI 48331-3535
Or you can visit our Internet site at
http://www.gale.com **ALL RIGHTS RESERVED**
No part of this work covered by the copyright hereon may be reproduced or used in any form or by any means—graphic, electronic, or mechanical, including photocopying, recording, taping, Web distribution, or information storage retrieval systems—without the written permission of the publisher.

For permission to use material from this product, submit your request via Web at http://www.gale-edit.com/permissions, or you may download our Permissions Request form and submit your request by fax or mail to: *Permissions Department*
The Gale Group, Inc.
27500 Drake Rd.
Farmington Hills, MI 48331-3535
Permissions Hotline:
248-699-8006 or 800-877-4253, ext. 8006

Since this page cannot legibly accommodate all copyright notices, the acknowledgments constitute an extension of the copyright notice.

While every effort has been made to ensure the reliability of the information presented in this publication, The Gale Group, Inc. does not guarantee the accuracy of the data contained herein. The Gale Group, Inc. accepts no payment for listing; and inclusion in the publication of any organization, agency, institution, publication, service, or individual does not imply endorsement of the editors or publisher. Errors brought to the attention of the publisher and verified to the satisfaction of the publisher will be corrected in future editions.

ISBN 0-7876-4899-X
ISSN 1094-3552

Printed in the United States of America
10 9 8 7 6 5 4 3 2 1

The Turn of the Screw

Henry James 1898

Introduction

Henry James's *The Turn of the Screw* has inspired a divided critical debate, the likes of which the literary world has rarely seen. When the short novel was first published in 1898, it was published in three different versions, as a serial in *Collier's Weekly* and in book form with another tale, in both American and English editions. James later revised the story and published it in 1908 in the twelfth volume of the New York Edition of *The Novels and Tales of Henry James*. It is the 1908 version that the author preferred and to which most modern critics refer. However, no matter what version readers encounter, they may find themselves falling into one of two camps supported by critics to this day. Either the story is an excellent example of the type of ghost story that was popular at the end of the nineteenth century or it is a psychoanalytic study of the hallucinations of a madwoman.

As a ghost story, then the tale details the classic struggle between good and evil and dealings with the supernatural. If one takes it as a psychoanalytic study, then the story emphasizes sexual repression and the sources of insanity. In either case, *The Turn of the Screw* has delighted readers for more than a century and continues to serve as one of the many examples of James's literary artistry, among such other notable works as *The American, The Ambassadors*, and *The Portrait of a Lady*.

Author Biography

James was born on April 15, 1843, on the edge of Greenwich Village in New York City. Born into a wealthy family, James was exposed to a traveling lifestyle. Less than a year after James was born, his parents took him and his brother, William, to London. A little over a year later, they visited Paris and then returned to New York, where they stayed for a decade.

As a child, James was not interested in school, and his education came periodically at day schools or from in-home tutors. People constantly surrounded James; his house was filled with an assortment of family, governesses, friends, and other visitors. Among the more distinguished visitors were writers Ralph Waldo Emerson and William Makepeace Thackeray. In 1856, James and his family moved to Europe, where he eventually fell in love with Paris and the French language. In 1858, the family returned to America, to Newport, Rhode Island. The stay was not long, and the family moved back to Europe again in 1859. However, a year later they once again moved back to America, this time to indulge brother William's desire to study art in a Newport studio.

In 1861, the Civil War broke out in America, and two of James's brothers left to fight. James, however, had injured himself severely—although scholars do not know how exactly—and could not fight. Instead, he attended Harvard Law School for one year, apparently so that he could get access to Harvard's library, literary social scene, and literature lectures. For the five years after Harvard, James stayed with his parents at home, which at this point was Boston, since his parents had followed him to Harvard. During this time, James, who had long harbored ideas of a writing career, began to produce his own literature.

His early writings consisted of short stories, reviews of other books, and critical notes. In 1869, James traveled to England, where his family's connections put him in touch with such notable British thinkers as Charles Darwin, George Eliot, and John Ruskin. He toured much of the rest of Europe, favoring Italy most. In fact, he started writing his first novel, *Roderick Hudson* (1876) in Florence.

James was such a prolific writer—important in the development of the modern novel—that critics have divided his literary career into three phases, based on the level of development in his craft. At the end of the middle phase, in the 1890s, James decided to experiment in a number of ways. One of these experiments, *The Turn of the Screw*, published in 1898, is a ghost story that has kept critics guessing as to the story's interpretation and James's original intent for more than a century.

During James's final phase, known as the "major phase," he produced the novels that most critics—and James himself—consider the novelist's best works. These include *The Wings of the Dove*

(1902), *The Ambassadors* (1903), and *The Golden Bowl* (1904). Although James was born in America, England was his adopted home for much of his life, and in 1915 he became a British citizen. James died of edema on February 28, 1916, in London.

Plot Summary

A Terrible Tale

The Turn of the Screw begins on Christmas Eve during the 1890s, in an old house, where a group of men and women friends are gathered around a fireside telling ghost stories. When the book starts, somebody has just finished telling a particularly gruesome tale involving a ghost and a child. Later in the evening, a man named Douglas comments on this tale, saying that he agrees that since the tale involves a child, it magnifies the horrific effect, which he refers to as "another turn of the screw." He proposes to top this tale with a ghost story involving two children, but when pressed to do so, he says that he must read the tale from the account of the person who has experienced it and that the account is in a book in his home in the city.

Over the next couple of days, while the group is waiting for the book to arrive, Douglas gives a short prologue to the tale. In this preview, he reveals that the story involves a young governess in the mid-1800s, who has been hired by a young man to take care of his niece and nephew. The one condition that the governess must adhere to is that she can never trouble the man about anything involving the children. Some of the other major characters are introduced, including Mrs. Grose, the housekeeper who is currently watching over the house and children; Miles, the ten-year-old nephew, who was sent away to school after the death of the previous governess; and Flora, the eight-year-old niece. When the group presses Douglas for more details, such as how the previous governess died, he is very guarded, preferring to let them make their own interpretations as he reads the account verbatim —which he does when the book arrives.

The Governess's First Days at the Estate

From this point on in the book, Douglas and the guests disappear, and the reader hears only the firsthand account of what the governess has written about her experiences at Bly, the country estate. When the governess arrives at Bly in the spring, she is a little nervous, since this is the first time that she has had so much responsibility. The governess wonders why Mrs. Grose seems to hide her eagerness to see the governess. The governess is delighted when she meets charming Flora. Her first night at Bly, the governess hears noises but does not think anything of them. When she goes to pick up Miles two days later, she is apprehensive, since she has received a note from his school saying that he is being sent home and can never return. When the governess presses Mrs. Grose as to whether Miles is a bad boy, the housekeeper is cryptic, as she is about the details surrounding the death of the previous governess. The governess meets Miles and cannot understand why anyone would dismiss such a charming boy.

Summer

Several weeks later, the governess sees a strange man while she is walking in the garden one evening. The man disappears, and the governess assumes he is a trespasser. The next Sunday, as the governess and Mrs. Grose are preparing to go to church, she finds the same man staring at her through a window. She runs outside to confront him, but he is gone. When she describes the man to Mrs. Grose, the housekeeper says that the governess has described Peter Quint, their employer's deceased valet, who was not a very nice person when he was alive. The governess feels that Quint has come for Miles and charges herself with the moral task of trying to save the two children's souls from being corrupted. Shortly thereafter, while the governess and Flora are in the garden, the governess sees a woman, whom she later guesses is Miss Jessel, the former, deceased governess. Although the governess swears Flora has seen her, too, the little girl shows no sign that she has.

The governess presses the housekeeper for more information about the two apparitions and discovers that the two were lovers when they were alive, and that Quint had questionable dealings with Miles while Miss Jessel had suspicious dealings with Flora. Several days pass, and still the children do not betray that they have seen any ghosts. One night, the governess sees Quint again, upon the stairs. She stands her ground, unafraid, and he disappears. That night, the governess finds Flora peering out of her window, but when the governess confronts her, Flora denies seeing anybody. One night, as she is doing her now routine sweep of the staircase, the governess sees Miss Jessel looking very sad, but she disappears after an instant. Shortly thereafter, the governess catches Miles out of his bed and wandering on the lawn, presumably to speak with the ghosts, although the children still deny any wrongdoing. The governess takes up the matter with Mrs. Grose, who encourages her to contact their employer. However, the governess is reluctant to break her vow not to disturb him.

Autumn

Summer passes into autumn, and although the governess searches for the ghosts around every corner, they are not apparent for many weeks. One Sunday, while they are walking to church, Miles asks the governess if he can be sent away to school and threatens to complain to his uncle if she does not let him. The governess is so stricken by this that she walks back to the house, intending to leave it for good. When she sees Miss Jessel sitting at her desk in her classroom, she resolves to stay. She also decides to write to their employer about the suspected behavior of his niece and nephew. Before she writes the letter, she goes to talk to Miles, trying to find out his experiences at school before he was sent home. When she pries too deeply, she suddenly feels a blast of cold air and the candle goes out, although Miles tells her that he blew it out.

The next day, Miles is very happy and offers to play piano for her. The governess is delighted at the music, until she realizes that Flora is not around. Miles feigns innocence over Flora's whereabouts, so the governess seeks the aid of Mrs. Grose. Before the two women leave to search, the governess places the letter to her employer on the table for one of the servants to mail. The governess and Mrs. Grose go to the lake, where they find the boat missing. After walking around the lake, the governess finds Flora and, for the first time, asks her bluntly where Miss Jessel is. The ghost appears to the governess; however, Mrs. Grose sees nothing and sides with Flora, who also says that she sees nothing and never has. Furthermore, she asks to be taken away from Bly, away from the governess.

Sickness and Death

The next morning, the governess finds out from Mrs. Grose that Flora was struck with a fever during the night and that she is terrified of seeing the governess. However, Mrs. Grose does say that the governess was justified in her suspicions of Flora, because the child has started to use evil language. The governess encourages Mrs. Grose to take Flora to her uncle's house for safety and also so that she can try to gain Miles's allegiance in his sister's absence. Before she leaves, Mrs. Grose says that the governess's letter never got sent and that it has mysteriously disappeared.

When the governess is alone with Miles after dinner, she asks him if he stole her letter. Before he can respond, she feels the presence of Quint and shields Miles from seeing the ghost. Miles admits that he stole the letter so that he could read it. When she presses him to talk about his experiences at school, he says only that he said bad things to others. The governess holds him tightly to keep him from the window, and he asks her if it is "she." She tells him no, it is "the coward horror," and the boy finally names Quint. When Miles looks to see the ghost, Quint is gone. Miles screams and falls into the governess's arms, dead, his heart having stopped.

Characters

Douglas

Douglas is the person who reads the governess's tale to the narrator and the assembled guests at the Christmas party. In the introduction to the governess's tale, Douglas offers to tell a terrible tale that heightens the terror effect by "two turns" of the screw, since it tells about ghostly interactions with two children. Douglas is very cryptic about his relationship to the governess, saying only that she was ten years older than he was and that she was his sister's governess, which is when she told him her tale. Once Douglas starts telling the tale, it is told entirely from the governess's point of view, from the account that she wrote down for Douglas.

Flora

Flora is the eight-year-old girl who the governess thinks is being tempted by the ghost of Miss Jessel, her former governess. When the governess arrives at Bly to take care of Flora and Miles, she is overwhelmed by Flora's charm; Flora is a model student in the classroom. When the governess sees Miss Jessel while alone with Flora in the garden, she believes that Flora saw the ghost, too. However, the girl sweetly denies that anything is amiss when the governess tries to question her in vague terms about what is happening. Even when the governess catches her peering out of the window in the room they share, Flora denies anything is wrong.

One afternoon, the governess realizes that she does not know where Flora's whereabouts. She and the housekeeper, Mrs. Grose, go looking for the little girl by the lake, where they see she has taken the boat. They walk around the lake, and the governess confronts her, asking where Miss Jessel is. At this moment, the ghost of Miss Jessel appears to the governess, but the little girl, no longer charming, tells the governess that she does not see the ghost and never has. She tells Mrs. Grose that she wants to be taken away from Bly, away from the governess. That night, Flora gets ill with a fever. The next morning, Mrs. Grose tells the governess that Flora has been using evil language. The governess has Mrs. Grose take Flora away from Bly to her uncle's home.

The Governess

The governess tries to save Miles and Flora from Peter Quint and Miss Jessel, two ghosts she claims she has seen. In the introduction to the tale, Douglas, who says that he was friends with the governess before her death, gives her background. The governess is a young woman during the events of her tale, and she has been given the task of taking care of Miles and Flora. The children's uncle has hired her on the condition that she never bothers him with matters involving the children. When she arrives at Bly, the governess is nervous, having never had this much responsibility. She is instantly taken with Flora and dismisses sounds that she hears her first night there. After receiving a note from Miles's headmaster that says he is being expelled, she is nervous about meeting the boy but finds him to be charming. It is not long after she arrives that the governess starts to see ghosts—first a man, then a woman. With Mrs. Grose's help, the governess identifies these ghosts as Peter Quint, the former valet, and Miss Jessel, the governess's predecessor. Feeling that the children's souls are in grave danger, the governess sets herself the task of protecting them from the ghosts and stands up to the apparitions on several occasions.

Media Adaptations

- *The Turn of the Screw* was adapted as a television movie and shown by the National Broadcasting Company

(NBC) in 1959. The production was directed by John Frankenheimer and starred Ingrid Bergman as the governess, Isobel Elsom as Mrs. Grose, Paul Stevens I as Peter Quint, and Laurinda Barrett as Miss Jessel.

- *The Turn of the Screw* was adapted as a television movie and shown by the American Broadcasting Company (ABC) in 1974. Directed by Dan Curtis, the production stars Lynn Redgrave as the governess, Megs Jenkins as Mrs. Grose, James Laurenson as Peter Quint, and Kathryn Leigh Scott as Miss Jessel and features an ending that differs dramatically from James's original text. The movie is available on video from Artisan Entertainment.

- *The Turn of the Screw* was adapted into an opera with a prologue and two acts in 1954, by the famed English composer, Benjamin Britten. The opera was filmed in Czechoslovakia in 1982 by Pgd/Philips. Directed by Petr Weigl, the film features Czech actors lip-synching the musical parts, which are sung by others, including Helen Donath as the governess, Ava June as Mrs. Grose, Robert Tear as Peter Quint, and Heather Harper as Miss

Jessel. Filmed in naturalistic settings, as opposed to a stage set, the opera is not widely available but is worth the effort of looking for it.

- *The Turn of the Screw* was adapted as a cable television movie in 1990, co-produced by Shelley Duvall. Directed by Graeme Clifford, the movie features Amy Irving as the governess. It is available on video from Warner Home Video.

- *The Turn of the Screw* was adapted as a film in 1992. Directed by Rusty Lemorande, the film features Patsy Kensit as the governess. It is available on video from Artisan Entertainment.

- *The Turn of the Screw* was adapted as a *Masterpiece Theatre* movie in 1999 by Anchor Bay Entertainment. Directed by Ben Bolt II, the film features Jodhi May as the governess, Pam Ferris as Mrs. Grose, Jason Salkey as Peter Quint, Caroline Pegg as Miss Jessel, and Colin Firth as the governess's employer—whose appearance deviates from James's original tale.

- *The Turn of the Screw* and *Daisy Miller*, two of James's short novels, were adapted to an abridged audiocassette by Dercum Press

Audio in 1987.

- *The Turn of the Screw* was adapted as an audiocassette and audio compact disc in 1995 by Naxos Audio Books. Both abridged versions are read by Emma Fielding and Dermot Kerrigan.

- *The Turn of the Screw and Other Short Works* was adapted as an audiocassette by Blackstone Audio Books in 1994, read by Pat Bottino.

Meanwhile, the governess keeps an eye on the children and attempts to get them to confess that they have seen the ghosts, too, approaching the subject in vague terms. When the children are unresponsive, she becomes more insistent, watching them at all hours and questioning them when she finds them out of their beds at night. She writes a letter to her employer to let him know of the suspicious activities at Bly, but Miles steals it. When she confronts Flora at last, naming Miss Jessel, Flora denies seeing the ghost and becomes sick. The governess has Mrs. Grose take Flora to her uncle's. When the governess confronts Miles about his association with Quint one night, she sees the ghost at the window. She presses the boy, who finally names the valet. When the boy turns to look at the ghost, it is gone, and the boy shrieks, falling into the governess's arms, dead.

Mrs. Grose

Mrs. Grose is the housekeeper at Bly, who gives the governess information about the identities and lives of Miss Jessel and Peter Quint. When the governess first arrives at Bly, Mrs. Grose seems to be overjoyed at her appearance, although she hides this emotion, which the governess finds odd. After the death of Miss Jessel, and prior to the arrival of the governess, Mrs. Grose—who is of a lower class than the governess—has been taking care of Flora, while Miles was sent away to school. Mrs. Grose cannot read, which the governess realizes when she hands Mrs. Grose a letter. When the governess sees the second appearance of Quint, she confesses the sighting to Mrs. Grose, who identifies the ghost.

From this point on, Mrs. Grose is the governess's confidant in the ghostly matter, although Mrs. Grose rarely gives information to the governess unless pressed to do so. Even then, she gives many vague responses, which sometimes cause the governess to come to her own conclusions. When Flora is found missing, Mrs. Grose and the governess go to look for her. When they find her by the lake, Mrs. Grose does not see the ghost of Miss Jessel, although the governess does. Because she cannot see the ghost and because the governess tries to browbeat Flora into saying that the child has seen Miss Jessel, Mrs. Grose starts to think that the governess is seeing things. However, that night after Flora has a fever and starts to use bad language, Mrs. Grose is inclined to side with the governess once again, and she agrees to take Flora to her uncle's.

Miss Jessel

Miss Jessel is one of two ghosts who the governess claims is trying to corrupt Miles and Flora. The governess is the only one who claims directly to have seen the ghost of Miss Jessel, which appears to her several times throughout the story. The first time Miss Jessel appears, the governess recognizes her, having already spoken about ghosts with Mrs. Grose after seeing the apparition of Peter Quint. Through Mrs. Grose, the governess also finds out that Miss Jessel, the former governess, was having an affair with Quint, who was much lower in class, and that Quint treated Miss Jessel horribly. When the governess and Mrs. Grose find Flora has stolen away to the lake, the governess sees the ghost of Miss Jessel once again. However, Mrs. Grose does not see the ghost, and Flora claims not to either, even when the governess presses her to confess her meetings with the ghost. After Flora becomes ill and is sent to her uncle's, the governess does not see Miss Jessel again.

Miles

Miles is the ten-year-old boy whom the governess thinks is being tempted by the ghost of Peter Quint, her employer's former valet. Shortly after her arrival at Bly, the governess receives a letter that says Miles is being sent home from school and that he can never return. When Miles arrives at Bly, however, the governess thinks the headmaster must be mistaken, because Miles is a charming boy. Miles is a model student in the governess's classroom and sweetly denies that anything is amiss when the governess tries to question him in vague terms about what is going on. Even when the governess catches Miles wandering around the lawn at midnight, he denies that there is anything wrong other than that he is causing some mischief. When the governess questions him about his activities at school, he is curiously silent; although at one point, Miles asks the governess if he can go away to school again.

One night in his room, the governess asks the boy once again about his experiences at school, and a gust of cold wind comes out of nowhere, blowing out the candle. Miles says he has blown it out, but the governess is unsure. The next morning, Miles is conspicuously happy, and he coaxes the governess into listening to him play the piano. When she realizes that Flora is missing, she thinks that Miles has set her up. The governess goes to search for Flora, leaving a letter to her employer—apprising him of the suspicious activities at Bly—on the table. Miles steals the letter, an act that he later admits to the governess. During the same conversation, Miles tells the governess that he got kicked out of school for using bad language. When the governess sees Quint's ghost at the window, she presses the boy to say his name. He says, "Peter Quint—you devil!" and then looks for the ghost, but he is gone. Miles screams and falls into the governess's arms, dead.

The Narrator

The narrator is the unnamed person who speaks in the introduction to the governess's tale and who tells the reader that he is reading the exact tale that was read to him, from an exact copy of the manuscript. The narrator disappears after Douglas starts reading the governess's account of her experiences.

Peter Quint

Peter Quint is one of two ghosts who the governess claims is trying to corrupt Miles and Flora. The governess is the only one who claims directly to have seen the ghost of Quint, which appears to her several times throughout the story. The first time he appears, the governess mistakes him for an intruder. After his second appearance, the governess's description to the housekeeper marks him as Quint. The housekeeper tells her that Quint was the former valet and was a vile man when he was alive. He had an affair with Miss Jessel, the previous governess, even though he was a servant and she belonged to a higher class. According to Mrs. Grose, Quint had suspicious relations with Miles while still living.

The Uncle

Miles's and Flora's uncle is the unseen employer, who, at the beginning of her employment, makes it clear to the governess that she is not to bother him about the children. The uncle never appears in the story and is only referred to by others.

Topics for Further Study

- In *The Turn of the Screw*, Miles dies at the end, presumably from fright. Research the known causes of heart failure in young children and discuss whether or not you think that it was realistic to have Miles die in this way. Use examples from the novel and your research to support your claims.

- The governess in the story believes that the ghosts, although they look like humans, are sinister beings who are trying to steal the children's souls. Research the views regarding ghosts during the nineteenth century in both life and literature and discuss how the governess's beliefs either adhere to or deviate from depictions in other nineteenth-century ghost stories.

- The governess is drawn to her employer, a gentleman who has a higher rank than she, and she makes much of the illicit affair between the previous governess, Miss Jessel, and Peter Quint, a man of much lower class. Research the various class titles that existed in England in the mid-1800s, from royalty to the peasantry. Using your research, organize the titles in hierarchical order on a chart, giving a one-paragraph description of each title.

- In the story, the governess assumes that the ghosts of Miss Jessel and Peter Quint are evil, and hers is the only point of view given. Put yourself in either Jessel's or Quint's place, and give a short plot summary that narrates the events from the ghost's point of view. You may choose to make your ghost evil, good, sympathetic, or any other type, provided you are able to use the story's events to back up your assertions.

Themes

Ghosts

Any discussion of *The Turn of the Screw* would be incomplete without addressing all of the major themes that various critics have identified in this ambiguous tale. The first and most apparent theme is that of ghosts. When the governess first arrives at Bly, she hears some traditionally ghostlike activity, the faint "cry of a child," and the sound of "a light footstep" outside her door. She pays no attention to these sounds, but a short while later, upon the second sighting of a man who she thinks is an intruder, she chases the man. However, as the governess notes, when she comes around the corner where the man was standing, "my visitor had vanished." When the governess sees Miss Jessel the first time, she notes the "identity of the apparition," using a word that is commonly associated with ghosts. The governess uses the word again when she sees Quint on the stairs, but it is curious to note that Quint appears "as human and hideous as a real interview," as opposed to appearing faint or ethereal, like many other traditional ghosts.

Good versus Evil

Even though the ghosts appear as human, the governess makes it very clear that they are evil and that hers is a fight of good against evil. When she is first talking with Mrs. Grose about Quint, she identifies the ghost as "a horror." Later, when she has learned the identities of the ghosts, she describes them, even in their earthly life, as "fiends." The governess decides to pit herself against the evil ghosts, noting to herself that "the children, in especial, I should thus fence about and absolutely save." Although, at one point, after she learns more about the children's relationship with Miss Jessel and Peter Quint during their lives, she thinks, "I don't save or shield them! It's far worse than I dreamed—they're lost!" However, the governess does not give up the fight, and at the end of the book, as Mrs. Grose is leaving with Flora to go to the child's uncle's house in the city, the governess notes her plan for Miles: "If he confesses, he's saved." When the governess gets Miles alone that night, and she does finally force him to say Quint's name, Miles asks, "*Where*?" looking for the ghost. At this point, the governess thinks she has won the battle versus evil, and says: "What does he matter now, my own?... *I have you* ... but he has lost you for ever!" However, after Miles shrieks and falls into the governess's arms, she realizes that, though she believes she has banished the ghost, Miles has died in the process.

Insanity

Could the governess be hallucinating? Besides actual ghosts, this is the other popular theme to which many critics point. There is evidence in the novel that perhaps the governess is seeing things.

First and foremost, there is the fact that nobody except for the governess has ever plainly stated that they have seen ghosts. The one time that the governess thinks she will be vindicated, when the ghost of Miss Jessel appears before her and Mrs. Grose, the governess realizes she has a "thrill of joy at having brought on a proof." However, the housekeeper does not see the ghost: "What a dreadful turn, to be sure, Miss! Where on earth do you see anything?"

The governess herself hints at the possibility of madness at other points in the narrative. When she is describing the state that she is in after the first ghost sightings, when she is watching in "stifled suspense" for more ghostly occurrences, she notes that if this state had "continued too long," it could "have turned to something like madness." The governess faces a much longer dry spell, in which she sees no ghosts, during several weeks at the end of the summer and early autumn. Although she does not describe herself in "stifled suspense," she does say that one would think that the lack of ghosts would "have done something toward soothing my nerves," but it does not. If one uses this and other examples of the governess's nervous condition, the ghosts can be explained as hallucinations.

Style

Setting

Bly, a "country home, an old family place" in the country, is a classic setting for a ghost story. When the governess first arrives, she is impressed by the "greatness that made it a different affair from my own scant home." When she receives her first tour of the place by Mrs. Grose, the governess notes the "empty chambers and dull corridors ... crooked staircases," and a "square tower that made me dizzy." All of these descriptions fit the profile of the classic spooky old house. So does the fact that the house features large, sweeping grounds, which include a lake and several pathways, both of which are imbued with the same feeling as the garden, the "lonely place" in which the governess first sees the ghost of Peter Quint.

Narration

Although the main body of the story has been written down by the governess, it is unclear as to when she recorded her story, since she notes in the story that she has "not seen Bly since the day I left it" and gives some hypothetical observations that might appear to her "older and more informed eyes" if she were to see it again. For his part, Douglas merely says that when she was his sister's governess, "It was long ago, and this episode was long before." Nevertheless, the governess has written the story down and sent Douglas "the pages in question before she died." As noted in the introduction, Douglas then reads the pages to the narrator and other assembled guests. Later, before Douglas's death, the narrator notes that Douglas "committed to me the manuscript," which the narrator is now telling to the reader. Because the story is from an exact transcript, the story can be assumed to be exactly as the governess wrote it down.

Because it is told in the first person narrative mode, the reader is called upon to trust that what the governess is saying is true. However, the governess has all of the traits of a classic unreliable narrator, meaning that it is unclear as to whether the reader can trust her or not. For starters, there is the question of how much time elapsed between Miles's death and her recording of the tale, as mentioned above. In addition, because the governess sees things that others do not and poses the idea that her sanity is in danger, the reader has cause to believe that perhaps the governess's viewpoint is not accurate. In fact, at one point, she admits to herself —and the readers-that she is attempting to "retrace today the strange steps of my obsession." The fact that her fight between good and evil became an "obsession" may have clouded her ability to tell the tale accurately.

Allegory

The good versus evil theme follows a specific narrative technique, known as allegory. An allegory is a second level of meaning in the story, which affects every part of it. In this case, the allegory becomes one of God versus the Devil, with the governess representing God-like or divine qualities, while the ghosts, and sometimes the children, represent Devil-like or evil qualities. The governess invokes the name of God on many occasions. When she has first seen her main opponent, the ghost of Peter Quint, she remarks to Mrs. Grose: "God help me if I know *what* he is!" A few lines down from this comment, Mrs. Grose says, "It's time we should be at church." Church is a traditional symbol of God, and indeed the governess looks to her church for strength when she feels she is starting to lose the battle for Miles's soul. She is on her way to church with the boy and thinks "of the almost spiritual help of the hassock on which I might bend my knees."

She also notes of Miles that "I seemed literally to be running a race with some confusion to which he was about to reduce me." At times, the governess describes Miles with demon-like adjectives, saying that it was his "wickedness" that got him kicked out of school. For the ghosts, the allegorical meaning is also clear. The governess uses terms of evil to describe them throughout the story, but at the end, when Quint makes his final appearance to her, she notes "his white face of damnation." She also remarks that, when she pulls Miles close to her to protect him, "It was like fighting with a demon for a human soul," a clear reference to the classical fight between God and Satan for human souls. Finally, when the governess finally presses Miles to name who "he" is, Miles says, "Peter Quint—you Devil!"

Historical Context

The Growth of Towns

The governess's employer, the uncle of Miles and Flora, is conspicuously absent from the story, always in the city, at his house on Harley Street. In Europe in the mid-nineteenth century, this was not uncommon. In 1800, London had approximately nine hundred thousand inhabitants. By 1900, just after James wrote *The Turn of the Screw*, the population had expanded to 4.7 million. For some, city life meant poverty, as the towns were segregated by class, with the poorer inhabitants living in slums. The more wealthy residents, like the governess's employer, lived in more fashionable districts. As the governess notes, "He had for his town residence a big house filled with the spoils of travel and the trophies of the chase." However, like other wealthy landowners who were able to maintain a second residence, "it was to his country home" that the governess is sent.

Sickness and Medicine

The nineteenth century saw many advances in the science of medicine—including a greater understanding of physiology and the use of vaccines and other preventative methods. However, since these methods were not always used universally and since medicine had not yet evolved into a standard, regulated practice, the effectiveness of medical attention was largely due to the individual knowledge and skill of the practitioner. People could not hope for a cure if they were to get sick. As a result, people attempted to reduce their susceptibility to even minor illnesses, which could develop into larger and more problematic ones. Between 1830 and 1850, people in Europe were especially cautious, as there was an epidemic of cholera in both London and Paris. In the book, the governess chastises Miles when she finds him walking outside at midnight, telling him that he has "caught your death in the night air!" Likewise, when the governess and Mrs. Grose realize that Flora has gone outside without telling them, Mrs. Grose is shocked: "Without a hat?" Wearing a hat to cover one's head, where much of the body's heat is lost, was one common preventative method to avoid getting sick.

The Governess

The idea of employing a live-in lady to teach children—especially girls—dates back to the Middle Ages, but became more popular near the end of the eighteenth century when the middle classes in England grew in wealth and size. However, the romanticized English governess familiar to readers of nineteenth-century novels like Charlotte Brontë's *Jane Eyre* (1847), Anne Brontë's *Agnes Grey* (1847), and many of James's novels has helped to instill the idea that governesses were common installments in every wealthy home during this time period. In reality, only a small percentage of women who worked served as governesses. For those who did employ a governess, the woman was intended to help the mother—or the widower, if the mother were not alive—with the intellectual and moral raising of the children. Like the governess in the story, who is "young, untried," and who is "taking service for the first time in the schoolroom," most governesses did not have any special training.

Compare & Contrast

- **1850s:** Cholera rages through London and Paris, taking many lives and putting many people on guard against illness.

  1890s: Because of better public hygiene, industrial towns have started to reduce the transmission of cholera and other contagious diseases. On a similar note, vaccines and x-rays come into use.

  Today: As modern medicine creates antibiotics and other medicines to combat disease, bacteria evolve, prompting the creation of newer medications.

- **1850s:** With rare exception, middle-class women are expected to fulfill their traditional role of bearing and raising children. For those who are unmarried, serving as a governess in somebody else's home, helping to raise other people's children, is an acceptable option.

1890s: Women work more and devote less of their lives to bearing and rearing children, and their expectation of life increases.

Today: Women have many options for both work and family. Some choose not to have children at all, whereas others remain at home, rearing their children and tending the home. Others pursue challenging careers in the same fields as men, and many balance both a career and a family.

- **1850s:** As a result of industrialization, cities increasingly become the center of business, and many English gentlemen keep city residences so they can better handle their affairs, leaving the hired help to watch the country estates.

1890s: In both England and America, the rapid spread of industrialization has widened the gap between the haves and the have-nots. The privately wealthy live in sumptuous estates, whereas many poor are forced to live in tight-packed slums in cities.

Today: Technology is a necessary part of many people's lives. Those who own and invest in these technologies become the new rich, whereas the poor continue to get poorer.

Critical Overview

James's *The Turn of the Screw* is considered one of literature's greatest ghost stories. Since its publication in 1898, it has been popular with both critics and the public. For the critics, the debate has always been sharply divided. When it was first published, the issue was whether the tale was artistically sound or a morally objectionable story. Many critics, like an *Outlook* reviewer, note both: "it is on a higher plane both of conception and art. The story itself is distinctly repulsive." Likewise, a *Bookman* reviewer notes: "We have never read a more sickening, a more gratuitously melancholy tale. It has all Mr. James's cleverness, even his grace." And a review in the *Independent* says that, "while it exhibits Mr. James's genius in a powerful light," the book "affects the reader with a disgust that is not to be expressed."

Those who found negative things to say about the book were often commenting on the subject matter, the damnation of children, which was a taboo and relatively unexplored theme at the time. A reviewer for the *Independent* expresses this feeling best, noting that Miles and Flora are "at the toddling period of life, when they are but helpless babes," and that through their participation in reading the story, readers assist "in an outrage upon the holiest and sweetest fountain of human innocence" and help to corrupt "the pure and trusting nature of children." Some early reviewers did purely enjoy the tale as a good ghost story, and recognized James's efforts to improve his medium. A reviewer for the *Critic* states that the story is "an imaginative masterpiece," and William Lyon Phelps, the stenographer to whom James dictated the story, calls it "the most powerful, the most nerve-shattering ghost story I have ever read," providing for "all those who are interested in the moral welfare of boys and girls an appeal simply terrific in its intensity."

For the next few decades, most critics continued to view the story as a ghost story, whether or not they agreed with the moral quality of the tale. However, in 1934, with the publication of Edmund Wilson's "The Ambiguity of Henry James," the debate was sharply divided again, this time into those who read the tale as the frantic ravings of a repressed woman and those who still believed it to be a ghost story. Wilson's assertion that "the young governess who tells the story is a neurotic case of sex repression, and the ghosts are not real ghosts at all but merely the governess's hallucinations," provided the fuel for the former viewpoint. Since then, the critical debate has been almost comical, as various people have come along and stated, with absolute certainty, that one viewpoint was true and the other was false. In 1948, Robert Heilman says, "It is probably safe to say that the Freudian interpretation of the story ... no longer enjoys wide critical acceptance."

In 1957, Charles G. Hoffman notes that "the Freudian interpretation of *The Turn of the Screw*

Critical Overview

James's *The Turn of the Screw* is considered one of literature's greatest ghost stories. Since its publication in 1898, it has been popular with both critics and the public. For the critics, the debate has always been sharply divided. When it was first published, the issue was whether the tale was artistically sound or a morally objectionable story. Many critics, like an *Outlook* reviewer, note both: "it is on a higher plane both of conception and art. The story itself is distinctly repulsive." Likewise, a *Bookman* reviewer notes: "We have never read a more sickening, a more gratuitously melancholy tale. It has all Mr. James's cleverness, even his grace." And a review in the *Independent* says that, "while it exhibits Mr. James's genius in a powerful light," the book "affects the reader with a disgust that is not to be expressed."

Those who found negative things to say about the book were often commenting on the subject matter, the damnation of children, which was a taboo and relatively unexplored theme at the time. A reviewer for the *Independent* expresses this feeling best, noting that Miles and Flora are "at the toddling period of life, when they are but helpless babes," and that through their participation in reading the story, readers assist "in an outrage upon the holiest and sweetest fountain of human innocence" and help to corrupt "the pure and trusting nature of children." Some early reviewers did purely enjoy the tale as a good ghost story, and recognized James's efforts to improve his medium. A reviewer for the *Critic* states that the story is "an imaginative masterpiece," and William Lyon Phelps, the stenographer to whom James dictated the story, calls it "the most powerful, the most nerve-shattering ghost story I have ever read," providing for "all those who are interested in the moral welfare of boys and girls an appeal simply terrific in its intensity."

For the next few decades, most critics continued to view the story as a ghost story, whether or not they agreed with the moral quality of the tale. However, in 1934, with the publication of Edmund Wilson's "The Ambiguity of Henry James," the debate was sharply divided again, this time into those who read the tale as the frantic ravings of a repressed woman and those who still believed it to be a ghost story. Wilson's assertion that "the young governess who tells the story is a neurotic case of sex repression, and the ghosts are not real ghosts at all but merely the governess's hallucinations," provided the fuel for the former viewpoint. Since then, the critical debate has been almost comical, as various people have come along and stated, with absolute certainty, that one viewpoint was true and the other was false. In 1948, Robert Heilman says, "It is probably safe to say that the Freudian interpretation of the story ... no longer enjoys wide critical acceptance."

In 1957, Charles G. Hoffman notes that "the Freudian interpretation of *The Turn of the Screw* can never be denied since ... the governess is psychopathic." In the same decade, Leon Edel shifted the focus somewhat, saying that the novel "has become the subject of a long and rather tiresome controversy arising from a discussion of circumstantial evidence in the narrative." Edel further notes that most critics fail "to examine the technique of the storytelling, which would have made much of the dispute unnecessary." Edel focused on the method of narration to illustrate that the governess is an unreliable narrator and concluded that it is the governess "who subjects the children to a psychological harassment that in the end leads to Flora's hysteria and Miles's death." In other words, another vote for a Freudian reading.

However, the traditional ghost story view did not dry up, and, as David Kirby notes in the foreword of Peter G. Beidler's 1989 book, *Ghosts, Demons, and Henry James: The Turn of the Screw at the Turn of the Century*, "the battle has been so even over the years that it looked as though neither side would prevail unless new evidence were gathered." In fact, Kirby claims that "Beidler has settled the issue conclusively; he is the new master of Bly and its occupants." Beidler, after reading through about two thousand ghost stories from James's era, uses his research to demonstrate that "the evil-ghost reading" is more likely. However, as Robert L. Gale notes in his entry on James for *The Dictionary of Literary Biography*, "the critical battle is still raging, and it is likely to do so indefinitely, since James seems consciously to have salted his text with veins leading in different directions."

What Do I Read Next?

- Although James was American-born, he was an Englishman by preference, and many of his stories, including *The Turn of the Screw*, take place in England. For other ghost stories that take place in England, a good introduction is *The Oxford Book of English Ghost Stories*, edited by Michael Cox and R. A. Gilbert and published by Oxford University Press (1989). This massive anthology includes forty-two stories, written between 1829 and 1968, from such literary greats as Walter Scott, Bram Stoker, Rudyard Kipling, and Edith Wharton.

- One of the most enduring English

stories involving ghosts is Charles Dickens's holiday favorite, A *Christmas Carol*, first published in 1843, concerning the famous three ghosts—The Ghost of Christmas Past, The Ghost of Christmas Present, and The Ghost of Christmas Future, along with the ghost of Ebenezer Scrooge's friend, Jacob Marley. Together, the three ghosts warm the frigid heart of Scrooge, who realizes the error of his miserly ways. A current version of the short novel was printed in 1999 and is available from Bantam Classics.

- *Voices of Madness, 1683–1796*, edited by Allan Ingram, collects four texts written in Britain in the late seventeenth and eighteenth centuries. All four authors—one woman, three men—were regarded as insane, and their narratives tell of their experiences, including their treatment by others. The book was published by Sutton Publishing in 1997.

- *The Legend of Sleepy Hollow* (1819), Washington Irving's classic tale of American horror, features a timid teacher, Ichabod Crane, who encounters The Headless Horseman, a spooky ghost in the backwoods of rural New York. The story is available in a 1999 edition from Penguin USA.

- *Like The Turn of the Screw*, which was written a year later, James's *What Maisie Knew* (1897) fell into the part of his career when he was experimenting with new writing techniques. In the case of the latter novel, James also creates a sense of ambiguity. In this case, the confusion comes from the thoughts of Maisie Farange, an adolescent girl who witnesses her parents getting divorced and remarrying, and slowly comes to understand the greater moral issues involved in all of these relationships. The book is available in a 1998 edition from Oxford University Press.

- One of the undisputed masters of the supernatural was Edgar Allan Poe, whose chilling tales have delighted readers for ages. In *Edgar Allan Poe: Complete Tales & Poems* (2001), one can see why. Along with the perennial favorite stories, such as "The Tell-Tale Heart," "The Fall of the House of Usher," and "The Pit and the Pendulum," the collection includes little-known works like "The Angel of the Odd," as well as

Poe's famous poem "The Raven."

- Through extensive interviews, research, and documentary photos, Leslie Rule's *Coast to Coast Ghosts: True Stories of Hauntings across America*, details some of the nation's spookiest locations. Written in a conversational style, Rule's book was published by Andrews McMeel Publishing in 2001.

Sources

Beidler, Peter G., *Ghosts, Demons, and Henry James*, University of Missouri Press, 1989, p. 237.

Edel, Leon, "The Point of View," in *The Turn of the Screw: An Authoritative Text, Backgrounds and Sources, Essays in Criticism*, edited by Robert Kimbrough, W. W. Norton & Company, 1966, pp. 228, 233, originally published in *The Psychological Novel: 1900–1950*, 1955, pp. 56-68.

Gale, Robert L., "Henry James," in *Dictionary of Literary Biography*, Vol. 12: *Realists and Naturalists*, edited by Donald Pizer, Gale Research, 1982, pp. 297-326.

Goddard, Harold C., "A Pre-Freudian Reading of *The Turn of the Screw*," in *The Turn of the Screw: An Authoritative Text, Backgrounds and Sources, Essays in Criticism*, edited by Robert Kimbrough, W. W. Norton & Company, 1966, pp. 186-87, originally published in *Nineteenth-Century Fiction*, Vol. XII, June 1957, pp. 1-36.

Heilman, Robert, "*The Turn of the Screw* as Poem," in *The Turn of the Screw: An Authoritative Text, Backgrounds and Sources, Essays in Criticism*, edited by Robert Kimbrough, W. W. Norton & Company, 1966, p. 215, originally published in *University of Kansas City Review*, Summer 1948, pp. 277-89.

Hoffman, Charles G., *The Short Novels of Henry*

Poe's famous poem "The Raven."

- Through extensive interviews, research, and documentary photos, Leslie Rule's *Coast to Coast Ghosts: True Stories of Hauntings across America*, details some of the nation's spookiest locations. Written in a conversational style, Rule's book was published by Andrews McMeel Publishing in 2001.

Sources

Beidler, Peter G., *Ghosts, Demons, and Henry James*, University of Missouri Press, 1989, p. 237.

Edel, Leon, "The Point of View," in *The Turn of the Screw: An Authoritative Text, Backgrounds and Sources, Essays in Criticism*, edited by Robert Kimbrough, W. W. Norton & Company, 1966, pp. 228, 233, originally published in *The Psychological Novel: 1900–1950*, 1955, pp. 56-68.

Gale, Robert L., "Henry James," in *Dictionary of Literary Biography*, Vol. 12: *Realists and Naturalists*, edited by Donald Pizer, Gale Research, 1982, pp. 297-326.

Goddard, Harold C., "A Pre-Freudian Reading of *The Turn of the Screw*," in *The Turn of the Screw: An Authoritative Text, Backgrounds and Sources, Essays in Criticism*, edited by Robert Kimbrough, W. W. Norton & Company, 1966, pp. 186-87, originally published in *Nineteenth-Century Fiction*, Vol. XII, June 1957, pp. 1-36.

Heilman, Robert, "*The Turn of the Screw* as Poem," in *The Turn of the Screw: An Authoritative Text, Backgrounds and Sources, Essays in Criticism*, edited by Robert Kimbrough, W. W. Norton & Company, 1966, p. 215, originally published in *University of Kansas City Review*, Summer 1948, pp. 277-89.

Hoffman, Charles G., *The Short Novels of Henry*

James, Bookman Associates, 1957, p. 71.

Kirby, David, "Foreword," in *Ghosts, Demons, and Henry James*, University of Missouri Press, 1989, p. ix.

"Most Hopelessly Evil Story," in *The Turn of the Screw: An Authoritative Text, Backgrounds and Sources, Essays in Criticism*, edited by Robert Kimbrough, W. W. Norton & Company, 1966, p. 175, originally published in *Independent*, January 5, 1899, p. 73.

"Mr. James's New Book," in *The Turn of the Screw: An Authoritative Text, Backgrounds and Sources, Essays in Criticism*, edited by Robert Kimbrough, W. W. Norton & Company, 1966, pp. 172-73, originally published in *Bookman*, Vol. LX, November 1898, p. 54.

Phelps, William Lyon, "The 'Iron Scot' Stenographer," in "Henry James," in *The Turn of the Screw: An Authoritative Text, Backgrounds and Sources, Essays in Criticism*, edited by Robert Kimbrough, W. W. Norton & Company, 1966, p. 178, originally published in *Yale Review*, Vol. V, July 1916, p. 794.

"The Recent Work of Henry James," in *The Turn of the Screw: An Authoritative Text, Backgrounds and Sources, Essays in Criticism*, edited by Robert Kimbrough, W. W. Norton & Company, 1966, p. 174, originally published in the *Critic*, Vol. XXXIII, December 1898, pp. 523-24.

"The Story * Is Distinctly Repulsive," in *The Turn*

of the Screw: An Authoritative Text, Backgrounds and Sources, Essays in Criticism, edited by Robert Kimbrough, W. W. Norton & Company, 1966, pp. 171-72, originally published in *Outlook*, Vol. LX, October 29, 1898, p. 537.

Wilson, Edmund, "The Ambiguity of Henry James," in *The Question of Henry James: A Collection of Critical Essays*, edited by F. W. Dupee, Allan Wingate, 1947, p. 172, originally published in *Hound & Horn*, Vol. VII, April-May 1934, p. 385.

Further Reading

Griffin, Susan M., ed., *Henry James Goes to the Movies*, University Press of Kentucky, 2001.

> In this diverse collection of essays, Griffin assembles fifteen of the world's most noted Jamesian scholars. The various writers discuss why James has become so popular to a wide variety of filmmakers, as well as the impact that James has had on film and the impact that film has had on James. The book also contains a complete filmography and a bibliography of work on James and film.

Lewis, R. W. B., *The Jameses: A Family Narrative*, Farrar, Straus & Giroux, 1991.

> This unique group biography offers portraits of Henry James's highly intellectual family, starting with the novelist's grandfather, William, in 1789 Ireland and ending with the death of the author in 1916. Through his shrewd business dealings, James's grandfather William made one of America's largest fortunes in the nineteenth century, which helped to shape the lives of the younger members.

McGurl, Mark, *The Novel Art: Elevations of American Fiction after Henry James*, Princeton University Press, 2001.

> At one point, there was no such thing as an art novel in America—and then Henry James came along. In his book, McGurl discusses how James's novels influenced the change in thinking that led to the widespread development of the modern art novel and then traces the development of modern conception after James.

Pippin, Robert B., *Henry James and Modern Moral Life*, Cambridge University Press, 2000.

> In this critical study of James's major fictions, Pippin argues that the author was motivated by his morals and that this theory of moral understanding permeated his stories. Written in an accessible, nontechnical style, Pippin offers new interpretations of many of James's fictions, including *The Turn of the Screw*.

Pool, Daniel, *What Jane Austen Ate and Charles Dickens Knew: From Fox Hunting to Whist—The Facts of Daily Life in Nineteenth-Century England*, Touchstone Books, 1994.

> This highly informative reader's companion is perfect for those who wish to learn more about the language, culture, and customs of

nineteenth-century England. As such, it serves as an indispensable guide to the fiction of James, Austen, Dickens, and other authors of the era whose stories are set in England.